Gussie the Christmas Goose and Other Stories

Terry I. Miles

AuthorHouse™
1663 Liberty Drive
Bloomington, IN 47403
www.authorhouse.com
Phone: 833-262-8899

This book is printed on acid-free paper.

ISBN: 978-1-4343-1961-6 (sc)
ISBN: 978-1-4817-5140-7 (e)

Print information available on the last page.

Published by AuthorHouse 11/29/2022

Other Stories Written by
Terry I. Miles "Cozy Little Murder Mysteries"

"I'll Love You Til You Die"

"Death Has No Appeal"

"Laughing All The Way" A Christmas Tale

"Say A Little Prayer For Me " (with pictures)

"DOG Gone Christmas " (with pictures)

"Looks Can Be Deceiving"

"A Catnip Christmas " (coming at Christmas, 2007)

authorHOUSE®

This children's book is dedicated to my three children,
four grandchildren and three great-grandchildren.
Also to all the children who lived along the
Mississippi Gulf Coast at the time of a most
devastating hurricane called, Katrina.

Table of Contents

Gussie, the Christmas Goose

Gussie lived upon a high mountain. Gussie's real name was Augusta. She was born on Christmas Day. She had soft gray feathers and a small beak. Her nose was colored with a slim black band. Gussie lived with her grandparents. Grandpa delivered the mail. Grandma baked the best cookies in the village and worked part time at the Village Hospital as a volunteer.

Gussie loved to fly with her grandpa into town. She liked to watch all the other geese take off. She always wondered where they were flying to. One day she asked her grandpa if she could fly with them.

Her grandpa said, "Be patient, Gussie. Your turn will come soon!"

Gussie could not be patient. She wanted to go right then! Two weeks before Christmas, Gussie told her grandma she had an errand to run for her grandpa. She had to go into town.

"Why?" asked Grandma.

Gussie blurted out, "Because, he asked me to." On the way to the village, Gussie felt bad. She had never lied to her grandma before. Then she saw the flock of geese. One by one they took off. Gussie was so excited! She started flapping her wings. Soon she was flying beside two older birds. "Hi, my name is Gussie. Where are you going?"

Both of the older lady birds squinted their eyes. "I am Marty and this is Billie. We are flying to America."

Gussie was busy flapping her wings. "Where is that?"

"Umph!" said Marty. "You haven't heard of America?"

Gussie shook her small head. "No, is it far?"

Billie laughed. "Sure it is!"

Gussie smiled. "Can I fly with you?"

"You have to keep up!" shouted Marty.

But, Gussie could not keep up. Soon she was flying all by herself. It was getting dark. She was tired and cold. She thought of her warm bed. She remembered her grandma's cookies. Gussie was lost!

Through the fog she saw lots of bright blue lights. Oh boy, she thought. I can land there. All of a sudden a big metal bird was coming straight at her. She dropped on the wet grass and covered her head. It flew over her with a loud whooshing sound!

"What was that?" Gussie shouted. She got to her feet and started walking toward a large white beam. It went around her head in circles. Nearby two black crows were eating corn by a bonfire.

"Excuse me Mr. Crows," Gussie called. "Where am I?"

"The name is Blackie," answered one. "You are in New York."

"Is that America?" asked Gussie.

"My name is Boomer," said the second crow. "I am Blackie's cousin. Yes, this is America. Where are you from?"

Gussie smiled. "Canada. May I ask you a question?"

Both Blackie and Boomer stared at Gussie. "What?"

"What made that loud whooshing noise?"

Blackie and Boomer rolled about on the grass, laughing. "That was an airplane! Haven't you ever seen an airplane?"

Gussie felt ashamed. She knew she shouldn't have lied to her grandma. She knew she should have been patient, like her grandpa told her. "I wanted to fly away with the other geese. My grandma and grandpa do not know where I am. I want to go back home!"

"You better fly north, then," said both of the crows, and pointed behind Gussie.

As she flew over the village, she saw her grandpa delivering some cookies to the retirement home. Soon she landed in her front yard. Gussie was so happy to be home. Her grandma was happy too. It was Christmas and Gussie was home for her birthday. That night Gussie and her grandpa had a nice cup of cocoa together before she fell asleep. Gussie decided it would be a long time before she would take a flying adventure again. She dreamed of fresh baked cookies.

The Adventures of
Doe-Denny and De-Doe-Denny
On the Farm

Doe-Denny and De-Doe-Denny were twin roosters. They lived in the chicken house on Mr. and Mrs. Barkman's farm. Doe-Denny was shorter and had long white feathers. De-Doe-Denny had reddish-brown feathers and a small black band around one foot. They were always getting into mischief. One morning Doe-Denny kicked over Mr. Barkman's milk bucket. Mr. Barkman chased him around the chicken house and chicken coop three times, but never caught him. When Mrs. Barkman came into the hen house to gather all the eggs, De-Doe-Denny frightened the hens and they broke all the eggs. Of course she scolded them and they were very, very sorry for all the trouble that they caused. Mrs. Barkman assured her husband they would grow up and become fine responsible roosters someday. Right now, however, they were just boys with lots of energy!

Several months later things had been very quiet around the chicken yard. Too quiet. De-Doe-Denny spoke up. "Hey, Brother! Let's go down by the river and catch some worms!"

"That's a great idea!" Said Doe-Denny. "When do we go?"

"Well, when Mrs. Barkman comes to feed the hens, we'll sneak out the gate!" said De-Doe-Denny.

It was late afternoon when Mrs. Barkman brought the feed pail out. Doe-Denny watched her walk briskly toward the fence. Slowly she opened the wire-mesh gate. Now both roosters kept their small black eyes directly on her. "Hello there, boys," she said, smiling. "How are you both today?" She began throwing the feed beside the hen house.

"Just fine, Mrs. Barkman," replied Doe-Denny. Carefully they both inched their small feet over towards the gate and freedom! As they escaped through the wire-mesh gate, Mrs. Barkman turned and saw what they had done. "Boys come back here! You could get hurt!" But it was too late. Both roosters were running down the green grassy patch. Soon they reached the river.

"Whoa, slow down brother, I'm tired," cried De-Doe-Denny.

"Hey look over there!" said Doe-Denny. "Isn't that a boat? Is this great or what?"

De-Doe-Denny hurried over. "Let's get in!"

They pushed the small gray dingy into deeper water. Both boys started paddling with the oars that they found lying inside the boat. Excitement shone on their faces. The water was getting rough. Ahead were the rapids!

De-Doe-Denny said, "Hang on! We will make it!" The water was cold. The two roosters were wet and tired. Suddenly this was no longer fun, for Doe-Denny had fallen overboard! Straight ahead was a hanging tree limb. It stretched over the water. Doe-Denny was going to grab it when he came close. The little boat traveled faster and faster. De-Doe-Denny extended his oar. "Grab on!" he ordered. Doe-Denny struggled to stay afloat! He missed! "Try again!" Shouted De-Doe-Denny. He caught the end of the paddle. Ahead were more rapids! De-Doe-Denny yelled, "Look out for all the rocks! I'll guide us through!"

This was more than they had bargained for. The roosters were tossed about. The crisis had passed. Now they were floating into a quiet lagoon.

"Whew, you scared me," said De-Doe-Denny, and then pulled his brother into the boat.

"Scared you? Hey, I was the one in the water!" Doe-Denny cried.

It was very dark and they didn't know where they were. Together they whimpered, "We have to get back to the chicken house!"

After pushing the boat over to the river edge, Doe-Denny and De-Doe-Denny hopped out and started to lie upon the soft green grass.

Someone was watching them from behind a small tree. Doe-Denny was the first to notice. "Who are you?" he asked.

It was a little red fox. "They call me Rudy, that's short for Rudolph. I live nearby. Where did you come from?"

De-Doe-Denny stood up and shook his feathers. "This is my brother, Doe-Denny. I'm De-Doe-Denny. We live on Mr. and Mrs. Barkman's farm."

"Is it far away from here?" asked Rudy.

"I think so, Rudy," said Doe-Denny. "Could you help us?"

"Sure!" Rudy said with a grin. "And my friend Bucky can help."

"Who's Bucky?" asked De-Doe-Denny.

"You'll see," said Rudy.

So off they went through the woods. A few miles down the road, Rudy called out in a loud voice, "Bucky!" A spotted bobcat jumped from a tall oak tree. "What's up, Rudy?"

"Hi there, Bucky. Meet my new friends. They're lost. I said we would help. Okay?"

"Sure," said Bucky. So the four of them went scampering through the forest. When night fell they stopped and rested at a small deserted cabin. In the morning they set out again, finally reaching the top of the hill. Below was Mr. & Mrs. Barkman's farm. Doe-Denny started running down the hill. De-Doe-Denny was right behind him. Then they stopped. "Thanks!" they shouted to Rudy and Bucky.

"You're welcome," said Bucky and Rudy.

They waited at the wire-mesh gate and just a few minutes later, Mrs. Barkman came whistling down the stone path, carrying her pail of chicken feed. She was thrilled to see the twin roosters. The twins were happy to be home!

"Well now," said Mrs. Barkman with a big smile. "I'm glad to see you are okay."

De-Doe-Denny nudged his brother and said, "That adventure should last us a long time."

"Doe-Denny smiled. "Yeah, maybe. But I was thinking about the Easter egg roll in the spring on the courthouse lawn!"

The Adventures of Howard the Hoot Owl Who Was Afraid of the Dark

Howard the hoot owl lived with his family in a big knotty oak near a deep blue pond in the golden meadow. Mother was a nurse, who always smiled. Father, a wise brown owl, handled the night watches at the factory. Sally, Howard's big sister, had sparkly bright red feathers. Howard was seven and named after his grandfather, Beakman.

One special morning Howard woke up and stretched his feathers. They seemed different. He looked in the mirror. He had grown tail-feathers! He peered out of his knothole window at the golden sun. Howard felt safe and warm in the morning, for, as everybody in town knew, Howard was afraid of the dark. Who ever heard of a hoot owl being afraid of the dark? All the young owls at school called him a sissy, everyone except his best friend, Sidney, the screech owl. Sidney lived in the second tree down the street past the tall skinny lamppost. He loved to hoot all night long.

As Howard climbed out on the big limb, his father spoke in his deep voice. "Good morning, Howard."

"Good morning, Sir."

"Today is a special day. Do you know why?"

Howard's big brown eyes grew wide. "No, Sir. Why?"

"Mother and I decided it was time for you to go shopping with her."

Howard began to shake. Shopping took all day, he thought. They wouldn't return until it was dark, very, very dark! His sister could go. She loved to shop. She was two years older! Her feathers were stronger.

Father wrapped his big wing around Howard's shoulder. "This will be your first long flight. We'll be very proud of you." Then his father laughed. "You know, Sidney hasn't got his tail-feathers yet!"

"Breakfast is ready," called Mother.

Howard started to turn around and his small feet slipped. Father quickly nabbed him by his small wing and pulled him back up. "There you go, Son."

"Howard, your breakfast is getting cold!"

"Coming, Mother."

His sister Sally was sitting at the table, nibbling at her cereal. "Why can't I go shopping, Momma?"

Mother answered softly, "Your little brother has to learn the trade winds and directions."

Sally started to complain.

"Now Sally, you behave yourself," said Mother while she placed Howard's eggs on the table.

"But he's afraid!" whined Sally. "He's always afraid!"

"I am not!" said Howard.

"You are too!" yelled Sally. "Mother still leaves your nightlight on!"

Howard's eyes filled with tears. Mother's eyes flashed! "Stop that bickering at once, Sally! Howard, what's wrong?"

"Nothing," he mumbled.

"Sally, dear, don't tease your little brother. You may need his help someday."

"Well," snickered Sally, "I hope he gets lost." She stomped out of the kitchen.

Mother sat down beside Howard. "Dear," she began, "remember these words. The light of the moon will help you out."

"Yes, Mother, I'll remember," Howard promised.

From above came a shout from Father. "Mother, come quick! Sidney's here. His mother broke her foot."

"I must go and help her," said Mother. As she started up the steps, she turned and looked at Howard. "Sally will have to take you shopping."

"Sally?" Howard asked, not believing his bad luck.

"Yes, Dear."

Soon the young owls were waving goodbye. The air was crisp. Howard tried hard to keep up with his older sister. She was flying so fast. When they arrived at the village Sally began shopping right away. She looked for bargains. Everyone needed a new coat because winter was coming. The family needed seeds and Mother wanted new medicines.

After several hours Howard asked, "Can we go home now?"

"Don't be in such a hurry," Sally ordered.

After shopping all day, Sally finally agreed it was time to go home. Howard looked up in the sky. The sun had gone down. It was getting very, very dark. Their beaks held drawstring bags filled with packages. They flew slowly, until they reached the forest outside the city limits. A dark cloud closed in. The wind began blowing hard. A loud bang of thunder sounded!

The rain poured down and soaked them. A sudden gust of wind caught Sally and knocked her to the ground!

Howard quickly landed beside her. "Are you all right?" he asked.

"I've hurt my wing! I can't fly.. .you must get help!"

"I can't!" wailed Howard.

"You must be strong! Go!" Sally yelled.

A lightening bolt lit up the whole sky! Howard could see all of the forest. His beak picked up different smells. He didn't have time to be afraid! Howard was very tired. He saw a large tall pine tree and decided to rest. Two yellow eyes stared at him. "Who are you?" asked Mrs. Eagle. "You almost hit my nest!"

"My name is Howard. My sister Sally broke her wing. I'm on my way home."

"Oh, you must hurry then," Mrs. Eagle shouted. "But be careful."

Howard saw that the rain had quit and the wind had died down. Now the large yellow moon shone bright. Mother was right. The moon would guide him home.

Father and Mother were very worried. The children were late! Father began rounding up a search party. Mother looked toward the full moon. There he was! Howard's form shone in the moonlight! Everyone cheered! Mother and Father rushed up where Howard landed. "We're so happy to see you. Where's Sally?"

"She broke her wing, Mother," said Howard. After Howard told his Father and the other owls where Sally was, they left the village to find her.

The next day there was a big celebration in town. Sally was back, safe and sound, and Howard had made his first trade wind flight. All the owls at school never called Howard a sissy again. Instead they had a new name. It was Howard, the Hero!

Andy, The Near-Sighted Alligator

In the back marshes of the Mississippi bayou, lived a family of alligators. Andy was the youngest alligator. His older sister and brother had been going to school for two years. Andy could hardly wait to join them. Finally the big day arrived!

As the three of them swam through the warm water, they noticed that Andy kept turning to the right when they came to a fork in the bayou.

"What's wrong with you?" His sister asked.

"Come on Andy, stay close to us," yelled his brother.

However, at the next boggy marsh, Andy darted to the right...again. Eventually, all three of them got to school.

When the three of them arrived home that afternoon, their mother had just returned from her job. She was a waitress at the Gator Café.

"Mom?" said Andy's sister, Sweetie, "something is wrong with Andy's eyes."

"Yeah," said his brother Al."

"It's 'yes ma'am,' Alfred," his mother reminded him.

"Yes, ma'am."

"Now, what seems to be the problem?"

"We think Andy needs glasses. Every time we turned left in the bayou, Andy would go right."

"Andy," his mother asked, "is that true?"

"Yes ma'am, but I don't think I need any glasses."

"Well son, your father and I will make an appointment with the eye doctor."

"Yes, ma'am," said Andy very softly.

The next week, Andy's father and mother took time off from their jobs and took Andy to Dr. Gates, the eye doctor. He confirmed that Andy was near-sighted and needed to wear corrected lenses, for at least six months. When the three of them returned home, his sister and brother began laughing at him. "Look," they said, "he has four eyes now!"

Father ordered them to be quiet. "You mustn't laugh at your brother because he has to wear glasses. How would you feel if someone laughed at you? Now apologize."

"We've sorry Andy," they said, and then turned their heads and tails, snickering.

The next day, the three of them started off to school. Andy had no trouble keeping up. His glasses were doing their job. However, when he went into his classroom, all of the other alligators busted out laughing and making fun of his little glasses.

"Children, please!" said the teacher. "You mustn't do this. But it was too late.

Andy turned and hurried out of the classroom and quickly made his way to the bayou. As he swam along, he took off his glasses and threw them into the marsh. Andy swam and swam. He was very, very tired. It seemed to be taking him a long time to get to the fork in the bayou.

Suddenly he heard a loud noise. He tried to figure out what it was. It was getting closer and closer. It was a lot of water, going somewhere. As he crept along, he realized he had taken the wrong turn! Now he recognized the sound! It was a waterfall! How had he gotten into the river? Quickly he began retracing his tracks, but it was useless! He was going over the falls!

Suddenly his whole body was turning in mid air. He felt as if his arms and legs were flying by themselves! Then, his small body smashed into the water below. As he sunk down, down, down, he thought of his momma and papa. He remembered his brother and sister and wished he hadn't thrown away his glasses!

Within seconds, Andy bobbed up to the surface of the water. He began swimming toward the grassy shoreline. As he wearily climbed upon the soft green grass, he heard a familiar voice. It was Mr. Gates, the eye doctor.

"Andy, what are you doing in the river? Have you lost your glasses?"

Andy swallowed long and hard. "No sir, I threw them away because all the kids made fun of me!"

Mr. Gates laughed softly. "So you decided to take them off. I see. But look what happened. They are still back in school, learning their lessons and you, Andy, are very, very far from home. But, I think you have learned a very valuable lesson."

Andy squinted his tiny black eyes. "You are so right Mr. Gates. I shouldn't have thrown my glasses away. Can you give me a ride home?"

"I sure can Andy. But first, let's stop by my office and get you some new glasses. Don't worry, I won't charge your mother and father."

As Dr. Gates drove into the driveway, Andy's mother ran outside. "Andy, we were so worried about you. The teacher called me and told me what happened. Where have you been?"

"I took the wrong turn in the bayou and ended up in the river. I went over the waterfall and then I bobbed up like daddy's little plastic ball on his fishing pole. Mr. Gates was on the bank and he brought me home. Momma, I'll never take off my glasses again!"

"Thank you Mr. Gates," she said and shook his hand.

Andy's sister came to the door and yelled, "Supper's ready, ya'll come and eat!"

After the blessing was said, Andy's brother poked him in his shoulder. "Hey, little brother, if I tell you something, you promise you won't squeal?"

Andy pushed up his glasses a little bit. "Okay, what?"

You know that little gray crocodile, named Carol?"

"Yes," said Andy.

"Well, she thinks you look cool in your glasses."

Andy smiled. "Really? Well now, I think I'm going to be wearing these for more than six months!"

Mr. Mouser's Trousers

"Hey Bobby," yelled Doodle.

Doodle wasn't his real name. That was a nick name his grandpa gave him. When he was a baby and first started crawling, he grabbed a pencil and started scribbling all over his grandma's white table. From that day on, everyone called him Doodle.

"Bobby?"

"What is it, Doodle?"

"Do we have to walk past old man Mouser's house?"

"Are you afraid of him?"

"Because.. .he's mean."

"Doodle, my dad says he's not mean. He just likes to be left alone."

"You mean he doesn't have any kids or friends?"

Bobby stopped walking and stuck his hands in his pockets. "My dad said his kids grew up and moved away. He had a dog, but it died last year. Ever since, he's been alone."

"Well...," said Doodle, "I still don't like walking near that old house."

"Okay Doodle, let's cross the street."

That evening, while eating supper, Bobby's dad noticed his son was strangely quiet.

"Bobby?"

"Yes, Dad?"

"Is something the matter?"

Bobby put his fork down. "Dad?"

"Yes."

"How well do you know Mr. Mouser?"

"Why? Has something happened to him?"

"No, it's just that Doodle is afraid of him."

Bobby's dad grinned. "Son, Mr. Mouser is okay. He's just older and is used to being alone. He's not someone to be afraid of."

Bobby's mother smiled. "Bobby, I happen to know Mr. Mouser loves banana pudding. Tell you what, I'll make some tomorrow morning and you and Doodle may take it to him."

The next day was Saturday and Bobby's mom was busy in the kitchen. "Bobby? I'm almost finished. Why don't you call Doodle and ask him to come over?"

A few minutes later, Bobby's best friend Doodle came bouncing into the kitchen.

"Good morning, ma'am," Doodle said.

"Good morning to you, Doodle. I asked Bobby if you two would like to carry this banana pudding over to Mr. Mouser for me."

Doodle backed up against the kitchen wall. "You want us to knock on his door?"

"Why yes, Doodle," she smiled. "I know he loves my banana pudding."

"He's a mean man."

"See Mom, I told you," said Bobby. "Doodle's afraid of him."

"Doodle," she said, "Mr. Mouser is not mean, he's just lived by himself for many years. Really, he's nice."

"Come on, Doodle," said Bobby.

Slowly they both crept up the rickety steps to Mr. Mouser's front door. "You knock," said Doodle to Bobby.

"Okay then," and Bobby lightly rapped on the door.

As the front door creaked open, a scruffy bearded man appeared. "What do you kids want?"

Bobby smiled and held up the covered bowl. "Hi Mr. Mouser, remember me? My mom made you this banana pudding."

Mr. Mouser's face began to change. A smile appeared. "She did? Well boys, come on in!"

Bobby shoved Doodle inside.

"Just set it on the table," said Mr. Mouser.

Doodle just stood there, looking at all the circus posters framed and hanging on the living room wall.

Mr. Mouser watched as Doodle's eyes took it all in.

"Do you like the circus, Boy?"

Startled, Doodle turned quickly. "Sir?"

"I said, do you enjoy the circus?"

Doodle smiled. "Yes sir. My grandpa took me last year."

"Well, my dog Checkers and I used to work in the circus."

"Really?"

"Yes, really. I was a clown known as Mr. Mouser's Trousers."

"Huh?" asked Doodle.

Mr. Mouser laughed out loud. "I pulled all kinds of things out of my baggy trousers. The crowd loved me!"

Bobby's eyes lit up! "Mr. Mouser, my little sister's birthday is next week. Can I ask my mom and dad if you could come and show us your tricks?"

All of a sudden, Doodle stepped forward and motioned for Mr. Mouser to bend down. "Since your dog is gone, you can use my dog, Taco."

"Why thank you. What is your name?" asked Mr. Mouser.

"My friends call me Doodle."

"Then I'll call you Doodle too. Bobby, you tell your mom and dad, I would love to entertain. You kids better run along and do your home chores. I have to 'get my act together' as they say."

As the two boys started back to Bobby's house, Doodle stopped and turned around. "Bobby, you were right, Mr. Mouser is a nice man, he was just lonely."

The next week at Bobby's sister's birthday party, Mr. Mouser and his trousers were a smash hit! "Bobby," said his mom, "just like I've always told you, kindness goes a long way." Doodle came running toward them. "So, Doodle," she said, smiling, "you aren't afraid of Mr. Mouser anymore?"

Doodle grinned. "No ma'am. Me and Bobby..."

"Bobby and I," she corrected.

"Yes ma am, Mr. Mouser is teaching my grandpa some card tricks!"

As Bobby's parents stood there in the doorway to the backyard, they looked at Mr. Mouser's face light up as he pulled all kinds of scarves, cards and streamers from his large baggy trousers. She gazed up at her husband and said, "Just think, all it took was a little banana pudding and a child's caring thought."

Printed in the United States
by Baker & Taylor Publisher Services